Danny
THE GUIDE DOG

Danny
THE GUIDE DOG

Jill Coleman

Photographs by Sally Fear

Hippo Books
Scholastic Publications Limited
London

For John

Scholastic Publications Ltd.,
10 Earlham Street, London WC2H 9RX, UK

Scholastic Inc.,
730 Broadway, New York, NY 10003, USA

Scholastic Tab Publications Ltd.,
123 Newkirk Road, Richmond Hill,
Ontario, L4C 3G5, Canada

Ashton Scholastic Pty. Ltd.,
P O Box 579, Gosford, New South Wales,
Australia

Ashton Scholastic Ltd.,
165 Marua Road, Panmure, Auckland 6,
New Zealand

First published by A & C Black (Publishers) Limited, UK, 1986
under the title *Guide Dog*

Published in paperback by Scholastic Publications Ltd., UK, 1988

Copyright © A & C Black (Publishers) Limited, 1986

The author and publishers would like to thank Carol Legg,
the Easton family, The Guide Dogs for the Blind Association
and all the staff at The Guide Dog Training Centre, Folly Court,
for making this book possible.

ISBN 0 590 70788 4

Other titles available
in this series:
Pang Pon The Elephant
Lloyd The Police Horse
Mist The Sheepdog

This is Carol with her guide dog, Danny, on her way to the shops. Carol is blind, so it is hard for her to find the way round busy streets and shops. That's why she has Danny.

Danny walks in front of Carol. He guides her around things which might get in her way and he stops when they need to cross the road.

Danny and Carol go everywhere together, even to the office where Carol works.

This is the story of how Danny learned to be Carol's guide dog.

Danny was born at a special Centre for guide dog puppies. Here he is at six weeks old. He is almost ready to leave the Centre.

Danny goes to live with the Easton family. They have a big garden and lots of toys for Danny to play with. Danny likes to chew everything, so his toys don't last very long.

Mrs Easton is a 'puppy walker'.
Her job is to teach Danny to be well
behaved. She starts by teaching
him to wait for his dinner. Danny
is not allowed to start until
Mrs Easton says so.

Danny soon learns not to make
messes in the house. He has to wait
until Mrs Easton takes him to a
special place in the garden.

'Good boy!' says Mrs Easton.
When Danny behaves well she
makes a big fuss of him.

Every day, Mrs Easton and Danny go for walks. Danny gets used to busy streets. He finds out about other dogs, too.

Danny likes meeting new people. He always hopes that they'll give him something nice to eat.

'No Danny, don't do that', says Mrs Easton. Danny is not supposed to ask for titbits. When he is a fully trained guide dog, he will need to think of his owner all the time. He mustn't go looking for scraps.

Danny soon learns to 'sit' and 'stay' while Mrs Easton does her shopping. But he is only a puppy. Sometimes he gets fed up and wants to go home.

Danny is learning to
walk on the lead.
A guide dog should
walk just in front of its
owner, like this.

Mrs Easton tries to show
Danny all the strange
new things which he
might see when he is
older. Here he is exploring
a telephone box.

Danny loves riding in the car. He sits on the floor at the front.
On trains and buses he sits under the seats, out of everybody's way.

Every month a lady from the Guide Dog Training Centre comes to see how Danny is getting on. She says that he is learning fast. He walks quietly on the lead and he knows how to 'sit' and 'stay'.

When Danny is one year old, he has to leave the Easton family.

This is Philippa. She is taking Danny to the Guide Dog Training Centre. From now on, Danny will live at the Centre and have lessons with Philippa.

Danny keeps practising all the things which he has learned. He will lie down and 'stay' until Philippa calls him.

When Philippa blows her whistle, Danny comes running. He touches Philippa with his nose to let her know that he has arrived. This will be important for a blind person who cannot see where Danny is.

Danny soon gets used to the Training Centre. Here he is being groomed by Mary, the kennel maid.

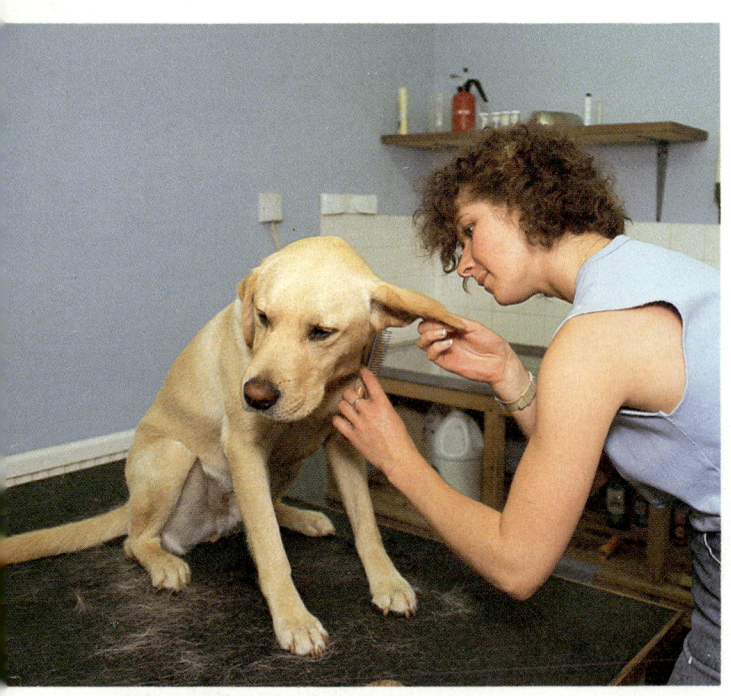

Now when Danny goes for walks, he wears a special guide dog harness. Danny learns that when he wears his harness, he is 'on duty'. He must walk in the middle of the pavement and not wander from side to side.

Danny is learning to understand some new words. Here, Philippa is telling him to go forward. Again and again, Philippa says 'Forward' and shows Danny where to go. In the end, Danny understands what the word means.

After a few weeks, Danny understands the words 'Forward', 'Right' and 'Left'.

Next, Philippa teaches Danny to stop each time they need to cross the road. At first, Danny doesn't understand. Each time they come to a crossing, Philippa shows Danny the edge of the pavement. 'Sit!' she says. 'Well done Danny, good boy.'

Soon Danny will stop and wait at crossings.
If he forgets to stop, Philippa says 'Sit!' and gives
a gentle tug on the lead, just to remind him.

When Danny is sixteen months old he has a new trainer, called Richard.

Richard takes Danny to a busy shopping centre. Danny is used to all the people and the strange smells. But when Richard tries to carry him on the escalator, Danny whines and struggles. Richard has to hold him tight.

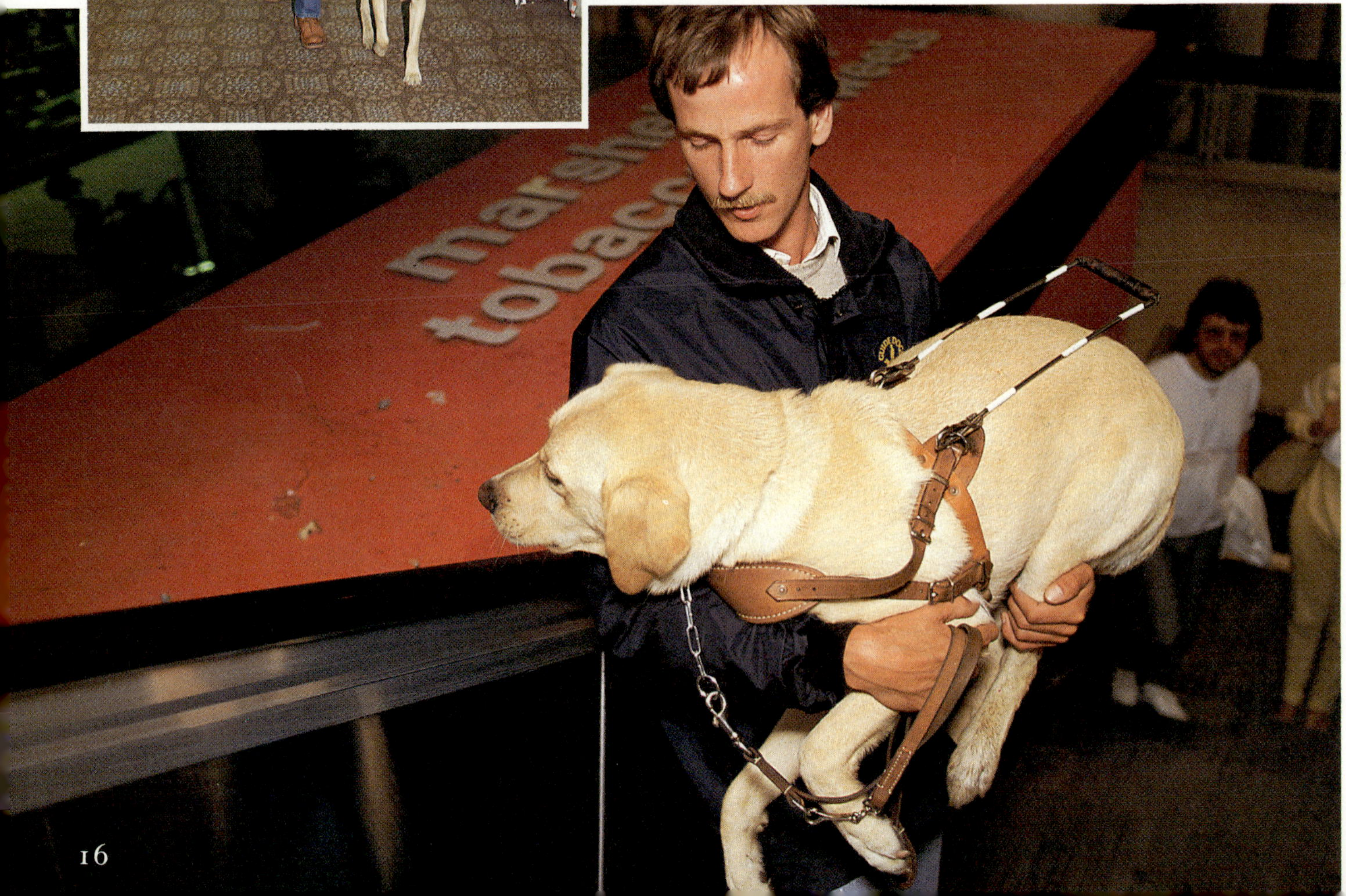

After that, Richard needs a cup of tea.
Danny still has a lot to learn, but for the
rest of the day he tries to be especially well
behaved.

In the evening, Danny has a long run with
some of the other dogs. They can rush
about and bark as loudly as they like.
Even guide dogs need to run and play
sometimes.

Richard teaches Danny to guide him around things which might get in the way.

Here he is, telling Danny to go round a post on the pavement. A blind person wouldn't see the post and might bump into it. When Richard holds the handle on Danny's harness, Danny knows that he must lead the way.

For extra practice, Danny goes around a special obstacle course. Here, he has to stop and wait until Richard says 'Forward'. Then he guides Richard around the obstacle and back on to the pavement.

Next, Danny learns not to go through places where a human couldn't go. He must always remember that humans need more space than dogs.

Danny knows that he must stop at every crossing. Then he must wait until Richard says 'Forward'.

Now comes the hardest lesson of all. If a car is coming, Danny must not go into the road. Even if Richard tells him to go forward, Danny must wait until it is safe to cross.

Richard and Danny practise over and over again. Another trainer from the Centre drives the car so that Danny can learn safely.

At last, Danny is ready for his final test. Richard wears a blindfold and lets Danny guide him on a long walk round the town.

Danny passes his test with flying colours! He is ready to meet Carol, his new owner.

Carol comes to stay at the Centre so that she and Danny can get to know each other.

At first, it's a bit strange for both of them. Carol has never owned a dog before. And Danny still thinks that Richard is in charge.

Richard shows Carol how to put on Danny's harness. Then they are ready for their first walk together. They go very slowly and stay on quiet paths.

Carol learns to groom Danny and to feed him. Every night, Danny sleeps in Carol's room. Slowly, they begin to make friends.

Every day, Carol and Danny go out together. They are learning to go along busy roads. At first, Richard stays close behind. But soon Carol and Danny can manage on their own.

Carol will stay at the Centre for four weeks. She will learn how to look after Danny and what they can do together. Then Carol and Danny will be ready to go home.

Richard will come to help them at home. But Carol will always be in charge of Danny. He is her dog now.

More about guide dogs

The idea of training guide dogs for blind people came from a German doctor who cared for soldiers who had lost their sight in the First World War.

In Britain, the first guide dogs were trained in 1931. Now there are several training centres all over the UK. They are run by The Guide Dogs for the Blind Association.

About half the guide dogs are labradors, like Danny, but golden retrievers, German shepherds and other kinds of dogs are also trained. Nowadays, the Association breeds its own puppies to make sure that they are hard working and friendly.

It is very important for the trainers to choose the right owner for each dog. A big strong dog wouldn't be right for a small shy person.

Do's and Don'ts. Don't pet a guide dog unless its owner says you may. Don't offer a guide dog titbits. It needs to concentrate on its job. Remember that the owner tells the dog where to go and when to cross the road, although the dog is trained not to cross if a car is coming. If you think a blind person needs help crossing the road, always ask first. If someone says they need help, let *them* take your left arm, then you can guide them across the road.

If you would like to find out more about guide dogs, here are some addresses you can write to.
If you live in the United Kingdom:
The Guide Dogs for the Blind Association
9 Park Street, Windsor, Berkshire SL4 1JR
If you live in Australia or New Zealand:
Royal Guide Dogs for the Blind Association
National Guide Dog and Mobility Centre, Chandler Highway, Kew, Victoria, Australia
Royal New Zealand Foundation for the Blind
545 Parnell Road, Newmarket, Auckland 1, New Zealand

Index

This index will help you to find some of the useful words in the book.